UMBRIA ON A WHIM

VOLUME 1: THE BASICS
AN INSIDER'S GUIDE FOR MOVING TO UMBRIA

Umbria
ON A WHIM

Tara OSH

Umbria on a Whim:
Volume 1 The Basics, an Insider's Guide for Moving to Umbria
Copyright © 2023 by Tara OSH

978-1-955541-08-4 paperback
978-1-955541-09-1 eBook

Library of Congress Number: 2023903790

Cover and Interior Design by Ann Aubitz
Published by FuzionPress

FuzionPress
1250 E 115th Street
Burnsville, MN 55337
612-781-2815
FuzionPress.com

TABLE OF CONTENTS

INTRODUCTION

L et me be straight with you, dear reader and possibly soon-to-be fellow Umbrian resident – this short handbook will almost definitely be insufficient in answering the many questions that you might have when it comes to relocating yourself, your family, and all that you know to a country that is not your own. It will also likely cause you to have even more questions than you might have had before. What is provided here as the first of the series could probably apply to any region of Italy - not just Umbria. It could absolutely cover a myriad more topics than it does, but no matter how much I try to cover it all there is no doubt I'd still fall short. After all, how can there be room for other editions or the full series if everything is in one book?

What I hope this book does provide is a bit of foundational information to get you started wherever you might be in your decision to make Italy, and maybe Umbria, your new homebase. I have tried to simplify confusing information for being able to get in and legally stay in the country. Other information is based mostly on our own experience, or those with whom we have spoken, which is hopefully more than a basic Google search can provide. It is aimed at those who are nearing 100% certain that the move is something you want to do, rather than trying to convince you to do it.

This is all to say that YES - it is possible to uproot your-selves without *that* much planning and live the *vita dolce*.

Therefore, please enjoy the following pages with their intent as a short handbook to help you get started with an Italian life written by a current resident in Umbria, **who arrived here on a whim** and a few other Umbrian expatriates, who have managed to survive the various stories they have shared here to make this area their home away from home.

Anything that is missing or not answered in these pages are open to suggestions for future versions or series pieces. Right away, I will admit that I intentionally avoided getting into the nitty gritty in anything related to the purchasing, renovating, or even renting a residence. That topic most definitely needs a dedicated volume that I shall endeavor to put together in the near future. With that, let's get to it!

WHY UMBRIA?

The more appropriate question should be *why not Umbria?* While many may envision Tuscany or the southern regions when they think of living in Italy, most are not aware that the same Tuscan-sun also shines on its bordering region of Umbria. This lesser-known province shares a similar landscape and climate with picturesque views that can be fully appreciated on a generally lower budget than that of its more known neighbors of Tuscany and Lazio (where Rome is located).

Although the likes of Rick Steves or Stanley Tucci have contributed to raising the profile of Umbrian destinations like Orvieto as a tourist stop; and the story of "Foxy Knoxy" nearly detracted visitors from the region's capital, Perugia, there is still a rather eclectic mix of part-time and full-time residents in the area with many a varied path taken that led them to the beautiful hill-top towns of the region.

This handbook aims to help inform (with an anecdote here and there) those who are looking to direct their own journeys, possibly on a whim, into a life of *Why not Umbria?*

◆ ◆ ◆

I have always been dazzled by Italy since my first visit in the spring of 1996. I was working as a food buyer for a large UK company, and I came to the Abruzzo area to source sun-dried tomatoes. It was all a delicious discovery, vibrant, glamorous, I remember thinking - Italy! Where have you been all my life? So began my love affair with the Bella Italia.

It was 1996 - a 'vintage year' in my life. I met and later married my husband, B. Late summer the same year, we chatted loosely about going on holiday and found ourselves in the travel agency, where B suggested the Lake District, but I thought, "Oh no I want glamour, romance, prosecco and people watching... Hello Capri!"

The 90s were also wonderful in terms of travel with the advent of budget airlines. We took full advantage of cheap flights to Italy from John Lennon airport. Often, we would take a £10.00 flight early Friday morning to Pisa, pick up a rental car and be sat in a piazza in an ancient hilltop town in Tuscany having a prosecco and daydreaming about how we would like to have a little home away from home in Italia one day.

One day was the future, an unknown point, perhaps retirement, certainly it was financially a long way off! ... For the next decade we traveled to Italy 4 or 5 times a year as often as work holidays allowed. Always a positive experience, Italians are somewhat special, their joy, spirit, passion, their sense of looking good, feeling good, having fun and generally loving life. It resonated.

Like love and death, illness can come uninvited and in 2006, I had a serious life changing illness which brought clarity to the meaning of 'one day' for me, for us. When I finally left hospital for the fourth time in 10 months, I had made my decision to move to Italy and our search started in earnest around the southwest corner of Tuscany and just over the border into Umbria.

In 2008, we discovered Orvieto, spectacular, charming, distinctive and enchanting in every way. For us it really was a ' Goldilocks ' hilltop town, one of the oldest in Italy and perfect for exploring on foot, not too big or too small or too busy, with beautiful winding medieval streets and flower filled piazze. Add to that exceptionally good road and rail links and being surrounded by glorious countryside with rolling hills, vineyards and olive groves; it was perfect for us.

We had already made a great connection with a local Agent and so we drew a 20 km radius around Orvieto and searched. In 2009, we bought our home on a hillside in Porano with wonderful views. I will be honest we didn't have a large budget and looked at so many unsuitable places we nearly lost the will to live, but this time spent in the area understanding the location was incredibly valuable, we met and made friends, enjoyed the calm simplicity and experienced a rural "hidden" Umbrian way of life and the region's culinary heritage that has remained virtually unchanged for centuries.

Although our home was a new build, it was only finished to first fix and so had no interior finishes like doors, kitchen, floor finishes. It took eight weeks to connect the gas, in which time I was so generously hosted at the home of our Estate Agent, Maria Laura who went on to be a long-term friend here. It was a slice of real Italian life with the added bonus that I learnt to cook pasta correctly!

B returned to the UK to work and I, having left my career, worked part-time on a freelance basis doing marketing for the estate agency and other projects and started to connect with trades people to work on the house. This was of course in the days before Brexit, and it took us six years to complete most of the house. Each spring and summer, I would return to Umbria and work would continue on the house; and each winter I would return to the UK while we worked and saved to create funds for the following year's works!

We had many fun moments ... Our Agent helped us with so much, for which we will be forever grateful, including opening a bank account. Banks are so very different in Italy to the UK ... There is literally no sign of any money! Usually apart from general transactions you need an appointment and on our first visit alone after purchasing our house, we were buzzed in and shown to some comfortable leather sofas to wait for our appointment. To our left was a glass office where the Bank Director was sitting. After a few minutes, the glass door opened, and the Director came over and introduced himself to us and then returned with a dish of Ferraro Rocher chocolates ... Just like in the UK - not! He had the most beautiful name, Giuseppe Marsala, a perfect example of the Italian "Bella Figura". I love how the Italians present everything in a tremendously elegant and graceful way.

~shared by M&BB

♦ ♦ ♦

While some residents will give credit to those mentioned earlier for planting the seed of possibility for an expat or immigrant retirement location, a common thread is: it was by chance, when asked the inevitable starter question of, "So, what brought you to this area in particular?"

♦ ♦ ♦

We were certain we were going to end up in Tuscany. Greve, Cortona, etc. But in the end, we felt like Orvieto was the best of all the middle Italy hilltowns. It was beautiful, big enough with a variety of restaurants/culture/history, and easy to access - perfectly located halfway between Rome and Florence. A few years after purchasing our home, we feel more confident than ever we made the right decision.

~shared by J&KN

♦ ♦ ♦

In the case of the author and my partner, we are English and American, and were originally planning on retiring in France as my husband – the Englishman – had always dreamed of owning a piece of land to grow some grapes and spend out his twilight years pickling his liver on his own wine. However, upon our first road trip through the Italian countryside, he took in the green of the rolling hills and felt its beauty. He turned to me and said, "Shall we just move here, then?" My reply was "OK, why not?" which triggered the process for our new Umbrian life.

Another British couple found themselves wanting to move abroad before the dreaded effects of Brexit kicked in and fell in love with the town and community of Orvieto.

Some part-time American residents shared that they just fell in love with the convenience of Umbria to places like Florence and Rome, but without the prices or city-mindset.

Thus, while the ways of getting to the region vary in uniqueness, a commonality is instantly discovered in the appreciation for the scenery, towns, and culture that leads them to looking for homes on a whim.

So, what are you looking for in your considerations on moving abroad?

VISA QUESTIONS

Before you take the big step of packing up your home and suitcases, you will want to consider your level of commitment to life abroad. Are you going to come and go throughout the year, thus just wanting a vacation home? Are you going to spend more than 90-days every six months in Europe – even if the majority of your time will be in Italy? Are you wanting to work toward becoming more or less Italian? Once you have an answer to these questions you will need to consider which type of visa you need to obtain.

Do I need a visa to stay/live in Italy even if it is just part-time?

The short answer is YES - for most people. The medium answer is YES - for most people. The longer answer is YES - for most people.

Unless you are already an EEA (Schengen area) citizen/legal resident you need a visa to live and/or work in Italy - YES, this includes you British folk now as well (Thank you, Brexit!).

Of course, as you may have gleaned from the answer variations above, it's not a simple matter of visa or no visa.

Let's see if we can outline some of the possible variations that may or may not require you to obtain a visa.

If you only want to be a part-time resident or just come for long holidays.

The general answer is that you can stay on a free/receive-upon-arrival tourist visa (assuming your country of origin has this agreement) for 90 days in a 180-day period (approximately six months) within the Schengen Area. http://bit.ly/3YCk5ib

This means that your work is not in Italy* (i.e., you do not earn any income from an Italian entity), and you are responsible to pay all income, residence**, or other long-term taxes somewhere other than Italy. In other words, for all intents and purposes you are on an extended holiday - lucky you, don't mess it up!

What gets tricky, and where this gets befuddled is, if you are planning on being a part-time resident, how the 90/180-day period is calculated.

Keep in mind that if you enter the Schengen Area **at any point of entry** regardless of if it is in Italy or not, the clock starts ticking. **The day you enter counts as a full-day** (yes, this is the case even if you pass through immigration at 11:59pm – we know some of you will wonder this!) and starts the 180-day clock that keeps ticking away no matter if you leave the country, or EEA, or not before those 180 days are up.

Furthermore, **the day you leave counts as a day** in the EEA, so don't go thinking you have an extra day (as in 90 +1 or 2 for travel). It's better to plan that you have 88 consecutive days to stay in the EEA - regardless of if you leave Italy or not - and two days for traveling directly to and from home. Any extra travel within the EEA needs to be factored in at your own risk. (You now can no longer claim ignorance since it won't help you with the immigration officers anyway!)

No matter when you leave the EEA (or Italy), your 180-day period must end before you can return again for another 90 (or 88) days. However, you could potentially come for 45 days, leave and return for another 45 days within that 180-day period - just don't forget to take off the four days of travel (there and back x2).

Is your head spinning yet?! Don't worry, you aren't alone. This is quite possibly one of the most-asked questions on social media platforms for those who are not quite ready or willing to commit to a full-time expat/immigrant gig abroad.

The key fact to remember is that if you overstay, you run the risk of being banned from the area for up to ten years, which could really screw up your long-term holiday home or retirement plans in Umbria! Therefore, **BE SMART and keep track of your time** in the Schengen Area NOT JUST IN ITALY! This is the most commonly recommended site, https://www.visa-calculator.com/ that can help you calculate your days.

If you plan to stay longer than 90 days, which visa should you get?

This is a complicated question and will require you to do some research based on what you plan to do with your time in Umbria. The information for this section is based on this site, https://bit.ly/3I1ONKc, but please note that requirements or options may change, so as with everything be sure to double-check with your local consulate or embassy to verify the accuracy of this information.

All of the visas listed below are considered a type of Visa D - or Long-Term Visa - which is really like a multiple entry visa that allows you to enter Italy on a non-tourist 90-day visa. You need to apply for this visa outside of Italy, usually in the country of your passport, though sometimes the last country of residence may be accepted if you are already an expat elsewhere.

♦ ♦ ♦

My partner and I have been expats for a number of years. So, although my wife is American, our last residence was registered in France. This became a little confusing when it came time to get our Visa D from the Italian consulate in Paris. On our first appointment at the consulate, we were told that my wife would have to return to America to apply for her visa. Obviously, during the COVID-19 period, this was not an option nor ideal. Luckily, my wife had been in email contact with someone else in that department of the consulate, who was unfortunately away on the day of our appointment. Therefore, we were forced to return a month later - the earliest new appointment available - with confirmation that she did not need to return to America and to just bring in some other forms. Thankfully, the second visit was a success and we moved to Italy from France a week later.

~shared by MF

♦ ♦ ♦

No matter what, the agreement with any of these visas is that you must **apply for a residence permit within eight days of your entry to legally reside long-term in Italy. I repeat - the Visa D (any of the below) is NOT the final stop, but only the beginning to ensure you are not overstaying a 90-day tourist visit. **

- If you have the means, you may live in Italy on an **Elective Residency Visa**, which is basically a "Retirement" visa. You must show proof of passive income (i.e., income from investments, pensions, - anything that is not a work salary) and a year-long private/independent health insurance coverage to prove to the Italian government that you won't be milking the social welfare system, which is designed for its citizens, who have presumably paid into it for years before needing to reap its benefits. This includes work - you cannot work under this visa. If you have the above and a few other required documents, this is probably one of the easiest visas to obtain.

- If you still want to work, you will then need to do a fair amount of research to ensure that this is an option on https://visaguide.world/europe/italy-visa/long-stay/work/ for you, but you can try for a **Work Visa**. It is not an impossible path, but it will not be the easiest one as you'll need to ensure what state the government is in so that it will want to offer you a work visa. This type of visa gets complicated and most recommend that you work with a lawyer, accountant, and/or notary along with your employer to determine your options. Some contacts are provided in the Resource section if you want to get in touch with someone.

- You may have the option of obtaining a **Study Visa**, but you must already be enrolled or have a promise of enrollment to an institution. Approved institutions should be double-checked with your local embassy or consulate, though probably language institutions like the University for Foreigners of Perugia, would be acceptable. https://www.unistrapg.it/en This visa must be applied for in your home country, so be sure to apply with plenty of advanced planning to ensure that you have your visa before your course starts. It should be valid for an initial one-year; and it is renewable depending on your course of study. A Study Visa holder is permitted to work part-time but be sure to check all the requirements beforehand.

- Another working visa option might be the **Self Employment Visa**. If you are thinking of opening a business (Startup Visa), making a hefty (500K) business investment (Entrepreneur Visa), or working freelance (Freelancer Visa), then this might be the best option for you that will last for a renewable 2 years. However, keep in mind that you will have to prove what kind of work you want to do, which means it will be a good idea to find someone in Italy who can help you to sort out the details required for approval of your work to ensure a successful application. You still have to apply from your home country even though this approval must be obtained within Italy.

Furthermore, there is only a set period of time in which this type of visa can be applied for, which is called the *decreto flussi* (flow decree) as there are a limited number of employment visas allotted per year. You will also need to get a *nulla osta* authorization form for the area in which you plan to work, register your business or work details. All of this can be complicated and frustrating if you do not have a good command of Italian; therefore, you might consider hiring someone to help you out as a local proxy. Also, renewal of this visa must be done within 60 days of expiry.

- For those who have family already residing in Italy, there is a **Family Reunion Visa** option. It may also be referred to as the "Italy Spouse Visa" or "Family Reunification Visa". Those who qualify for this visa are partners, dependent children under 18, or those over 18 who cannot care for themselves, and elderly parents (over 65) who have no other children who can care for them. It is important to note that the current family member residing in Italy must apply for a *nulla*, which (if approved) will then be forwarded to the respective consulate or embassy office at which the family member(s) will be applying for their visa to join the Italy-based member.

This application must also be done in the home country; however, there is a "Family Cohesion Visa" option in which everyone enters Italy at the same time and applies for residency under this visa option. If you choose this option, be sure all of your documentation is in order to avoid future complications. Those under this visa may work and enroll in school.

- Finally, there is the **Working Holiday Visa** if you are from Australia, Canada*, New Zealand or South Korea and are between the ages of 18 - 30 (*35). There are only 1,000 of these visas offered each year and allow one to work for six months, but only 3 months for one employer. Once you arrive in Italy under this visa, then you have 20 days to find a job and your employer must make the proper applications to fall under the appropriate permissions.

- At the time of writing this, there had been talk about a **Digital Nomad Visa** being offered, but with the current government status, this visa has been put on the back burner. However, if there is any change in the future, an update will be added here.

Here is a summary of the average duration and renewability for the above visas:

Visa Type	Length of Visa	Renewable
Work Visa	Length of contract up to 2 years	up to 5 years
Elective Residency	1 or 2 years initially	upon 5 years eligible for permanent residency; upon 10 years with permanent residency (total 15 years) eligible for citizenship
Study Visa	1 year initially	duration of your course of study based on the passing of all exams
Self-Employment Visa	2 years initially	application must be made within 60 days of expiry
Working Holiday Visa	up to 1 year	

Should I use a company or do it myself?

Keep in mind that if you already know Italian and have a high patience threshold, then doing the paperwork and wading through the visa process on your own will cost you less than 300 euros or so. However, if you find yourself breaking out in a sweat or itching from stress-rash, then finding a lawyer and/or notary who can help you may save on future medical costs from stress, or liver deterioration. There are other VIP companies that will offer hand-holding services that may make your transition to Italian life seem like you've moved up the social ladder – and who wouldn't want to experience that if your budget allows?

No matter how you choose to go about sorting the visa process, do your research! Online social media groups can also be helpful or get in touch with the author if you would like more personal help.

BUREAUCRACY

If you are a newbie to the world of expat living, then you may want to take up meditation or mindfulness practice focusing on breathing and calming the mind to lower blood pressure or the inevitable blow up. Bureaucracy anywhere is trying in the best of times and requires a Zen-like manner in the worst. Hopefully, the following information will help to inform you of, at least, the basics to alleviate stress sourced from not knowing what is going on or what to expect.

Codice Fiscale (Fiscal codes)

The *codice fiscale* is a tax code/number that is something similar to a US Social Security Number (SSN/TIN) or British National Insurance (NI) Number. Everyone needs one if you plan to purchase property, make money transfers locally, get a SIM card or phone contract, order items online for delivery, open a local bank account, etc. While there is some downplay on its importance according to some online sites, it is not a difficult process to obtain one, and many things are difficult without one, so I recommend that you get your *codice fiscale* as early in your immigration process as possible. Besides, it is probably the only requirement that will be free to apply and receive.

This linked site guides you through the fairly straightforward process of getting a code. Alternatively, most consulate or embassy sites will have an option for you to apply online / via email, so check their pages first. http://bit.ly/3KkmObw.

As this is one of the things you can most definitely do from abroad, I again recommend putting this high on your to-do list to simplify future processes.

Card or no card?

For the most part, you do not need the physical card. Since a potential wait of 45 days or more is often not an option for most people, the simplest way to apply is via email with the required forms and documents attached. If visiting a local embassy/consulate is easy enough, then you can apply there in person or they may recommend doing it online. Once you are ready to do the things that might require the *codice fiscale*, you can generally just show a photocopy / image of the code for most activities. The *codice fiscale* will also be written on your identity card later, so there really is no need to go through the extra step of getting a separate card at this point.

You may also find this article on https://bit.ly/3S9O2DDv helpful in learning more about how to obtain your *codice fiscale*.

Permesso di Soggiorno / Carta di Soggiorno (Permission/Card to Stay)

As mentioned in the section on Visas, everyone who plans to live in Italy for longer than 90-days needs to apply for a *permesso di soggiorno* (permission to stay) within eight days of your arrival. While you can use one of the various "hand-holding" companies that offer to help you with the process, it **is** possible to do this yourself if you are somewhat comfortable speaking Italian, feel a glutton for challenge, have a fair amount of patience and are ready to add another story to your adventure of making Italy your home – who knows, you might even have a story to share in future editions or volumes of this handbook!

There is a non-profit organization that may be able to help you as well, but like with just about everything, you may need to do some research and apply patience with an adventurous attitude.

First, let's cover the difference between the *permesso* (permission) and the *carta* (card).

Except for EU citizens and pre-Brexit residents, the *carta di soggiorno* (residence card) is a five-year-plus process for foreigners living in Italy to obtain. In other words, since 2007 the majority of long-term residents are now required to obtain a *permesso,* or permission to stay residency, rather than a *carta,* and renew it for up to five years, depending on the visa type. Once the five years have been successfully renewed, then residents are eligible to receive the *carta,* also called permanent residency.

Clear as mud? - Welcome to Italy!

Hopefully, now you at least have a general idea of the differences as the terminology is important only as it relates to the bureaucracy, but it also helps to know what you are actually getting when you start to settle into your new Italian life.

For the actual application, there are a number of websites and explanations of what you need to do if you are going to undertake the process on your own - i.e., without a hand-holding service.

These two websites seem to be the most helpful in English.

- An American in Rome http://bit.ly/3lLk4d5
- Italia Hello http://bit.ly/3KgXZ0m

Since each commune, city, or region may have its own process, it is always best to consult someone with experience in the area you want to settle.

Finally, if you find yourself satisfactorily through the process and want to check on its status, this site supposedly tracks your progress and can help let you know when it might be time to start kicking up a fuss to get your *permesso* cards in hand. http://bit.ly/3Z2Y9wp

Identity Cards

Once you have received your *permesso di soggiorno* (PDS), you should register at your local commune to receive your *carta di identità* (identity card). This will serve as your form of identification for most things, so if you are prone to losing your cards, you can leave your *permesso* at home if you aren't traveling across borders.

To obtain your *carta di identità,* or now the electronic (*elettronica*) identity card (CIE), you need to visit the commune office of where you are a registered resident. They will ask for various forms of documentation that is less cumbersome than that needed for your *permesso*, and if you've just recently made your PDS application then you'll have all the paperwork ready anyway - **so this is your reminder to make lots of copies of EVERYTHING!** Once you have completed the processing, keep all the paperwork they give to you as you will need the PIN and PUK codes that get printed on the papers they provide. Then, it usually takes about a week or so for the cards to arrive in the mail with the other half of the numbers that you need to login online or via the app, which gives you access to various services that will become pertinent as you settle in.

https://www.cartaidentita.interno.gov.it/en/cie/

So far, other than using it as a form of ID, I have not had to use the cards much, but it is handy if the *polizia/carabinieri* decide to do a spot check on the train platforms, for example.

DRIVING IN ITALY

Patente B di guida (Driver's License Category B)

Unfortunately, if you are a non-EU citizen and post-Brexit resident (*recent reports suggest that now UK citizens can do a direct swap, but do confirm before taking my word for it), you have very few options for obtaining an Italian driver's license that will not involve taking the theory test, at least six hours of lessons, and the practical test - *in Italian*. Yes, that's right, IN ITALIAN! There is no English version for any part of the licensing process in this region of the country.

While it is not impossible to find some workarounds to transferring a license over, there are no easy paths to a local *patente B di guida*. So, buckle up and prepare for the ride.

Fortunately, for those who are part-time residents, you can get by with having an International Driving Permit (IDL - *certificato di guida internazionale*) that is either valid for one-year or three-years for car rentals or short-term hires accompanying your valid home country license. In the US, these can generally be obtained from your local AAA office or possibly the DMV. In the UK, these can be obtained from your local post office. Any tourist or short-term visitor/resident can get by with the IDL as long as you remember to stay updated - not having this is NOT an option.

Unfortunately, for everyone else, it is expected that upon being a resident for one year you will have obtained an Italian license. This doesn't mean, wait for the year to be up, but rather that within the first year, you should be working toward getting your *patente B di guida*.

There are some states in the US that have reciprocity agreements whereby the US license can be simply converted to an Italian one by submitting the required documents and easily being issued your *patente B di guida*. Note that even a simple conversion can take a couple of months. For those who are not so lucky it is said that it takes at least six months to go through the process, but for most it takes longer so make sure this is the top of your priority list to get done when you settle in because you cannot drive without an Italian license once you are considered a resident. If you are used to being able to drive whenever you want, you definitely do not want to lose this privilege by being caught without.

From the start, you have two options: 1. Register at a local *scuola guida* (driving school); 2. Register at your *Ufficio della Motorizzazione Civile* (Agency of Ministry of Transport). Choosing option 1 may cost a bit more, but the school will help you with all of the process, which may be the best way to reduce the stress involved with having to study and prepare for the tests in Italian, if you're not already fluent. Choosing option 2 might give you more satisfaction and better stories when you have successfully obtained your license, though you may also have more grey hair and tear bags from the joy of dealing with local government processes. It's completely up to you!

Sadly, there is NO ENGLISH option for any of the tests required in this province. Going through a driving school may help you with the process itself, as they may speak English; however, the tests - both theory and practical - will be in Italian. You can still study for the theory test in English, but it is best to have the Italian version as well to memorize the terminology used for the actual test as with most formalized exams, wording is purposely tricky to ensure understanding.

This article may be helpful https://bit.ly/3xwSEdA in getting you started with apps and useful sites to begin your driving license process.

If you have an EU issued license (even if you are not a citizen), then you may drive without obtaining an Italian license as long as you maintain its validity. If you plan to reside full-time in Italy, then it is recommended that you still convert your license to a local one.

**It is also important to be aware of the fact that once you have obtained your driving license through the full process, there is a three-year newly licensed driver (*neopatentato*) period in which you are not allowed to drive a vehicle more than 55 Kw/t or at speeds faster than 100 km/h on the highways and 90 km/h on the motorways. **

Car Insurance (*carta verde*) and Ownership

Technically, you do not have to have an Italian license to purchase a car, but you may need it to insure the car, which is a requirement.

Even if you are driving your own car from another country, you need to have it insured before arriving in Italy for 15-45 days. Therefore, be sure to check with your insurance company before embarking on your road trip and check for *rinuncia al diritto di rivalsa*, which insures the driver and the owner of the vehicle in question. For anything longer than 45 days in the country, the car and insurance need to be registered with a local Italian provider.

To own a car in Italy, you must have residency. While some bring over cars from other countries, it is legally required that they return to the original country within the 45-day period. Otherwise, it is necessary to register the car in Italy with insurance as a resident.

◆ ◆ ◆

It is not impossible to get your license. After studying and retaking the written test multiple times, I was able to finally pass it in Italian, even though my language skills are not up to par. Even though I would feel discouraged after each failure, I did not have a choice as I live in a small town where a car is a must. Since I have been driving for many years, the practical test was fine once I practiced the roundabouts and commands with the driving school. All I can say is, don't give up and although there may be frustrating moments, the satisfaction of getting the license is so worth it!

~shared by TM

◆ ◆ ◆

Health Insurance

While some visa types require you to show proof of a year's health coverage, you may still opt to register for local health insurance once you are an approved resident. No matter what long-term visa you are living in Umbria under, you are eligible to register for local healthcare. However, if you are under a short-term or tourist visa, then this section is NOT for you and you should acquire travel insurance from your home country.

Before you can visit any medical offices outside of an Emergency Room, you need to register with the National Health Service (SSN) to be assigned a general practitioner, which means you will need to go through a few more hoops to sign up for the local health insurance. Voluntary registration is based on the calendar year and covers you upon an upfront flat-rate contribution. This flat rate is calculated based upon your total earned income the previous year whether in Italy or not.

A summarized calculation is:
- If your income is at least 21,000** (estimated) euros annually then 7.5% is charged; making your contribution amount equal to about 1,575 euros for the year.
- If your income is between 21k and 52k** euros, then 4% is charged. If you make more than 52k euros, then you will only be charged 2,080 euros for the year - regardless.

Therefore, the most you need to pay for the health insurance is 2,080** euros upfront for the entire year. The least amount for non-students or au pairs is about 388** euros. In other words, students and au pairs get further considerations that could require an even lower payment of around 150 to 220** euros.

***These are all subject to change depending on the Italian government decisions. ***

This site may be helpful in getting you started on this process. http://bit.ly/3Ec9dPx

If you are coming to Italy with specific health care needs, this may provide some relevant information on how to go about preparing for your treatment; https://bit.ly/418fy8S however, make note that it does not mean that you are not liable for any and all payments.

If you are waiting for your *permesso*, you can still register with your nearest *Unità/Aziende Sanitarie Locali* (U/ASL - local health authority) using your *codice fiscale*. However, you will not receive your health card until you are approved for residency; therefore, you may want to wait to do this step after you have received your *permesso*. Make note that if you have moved or changed addresses in the time of your *permesso* registration and when you visit the ASL, you will need to confirm your newest address BEFORE you register for the SSN as your *tessera sanitaria* (health card) will be mailed to your government system registered address.

For more details about what the *tessera sanitaria* can do for you, check out this document. https://bit.ly/3IGJKAN

◆　◆　◆

Umbria is a welcoming place in all aspects. The health care system at first seems like it's from ancient times, old buildings, old machinery, old doctors who don't speak English. Yet, once you need the system, you begin to feel the compassion of those within it.

The hospital is very good. It is clean and the doctors understand the whole status quo. The emergency services are free and available to all tourists and new residents.

The equipment at the hospital in Orvieto is modern, offering a wide range of departments.

Having been to the ER in Orvieto and in Rome, I would definitely consider Orvieto the better place. The waiting room is clean and has coffee/tea facilities if required. The hospital is

busy, but unlike Rome, which feels more like a cattle market.

The service in Orvieto is efficient. You can get most medicines as you would anywhere else in the world.

Generally, the Umbrian Medical services are equal to other places. My only criticism is the lack of doctors who speak English, which can prove difficult especially when not feeling at your best.

Still, I would say Umbria is a place worth investing time and energy in without serious worry about medical care.

~shared by RRS

♦ ♦ ♦

HOUSING

L et me start this section with a disclaimer that a future volume *Buying A House* is already planned for this series. In that volume, I will endeavor to go into detail about many of the ins and outs of buying a house in the region. Therefore, this volume will merely graze the topic as it relates to getting your visas where housing contracts might be required.

Rental Contracts

Some of the long-term visas may require that you show proof of a housing or rental contract for at least a year to confirm your seriousness in becoming a full-time resident of Italy. In some cases, an Airbnb might be sufficient in meeting this requirement, but in others you may need to actually find something of your "own" to rent initially before buying.

There are some options where a seller may offer you the option of 'rent-to-buy', which is convenient when it comes to putting down an address and having to avoid changing your address, commune, and documents later down the road. However, hopefully by now, you are no longer afraid of the bureaucracy and will not let such an obstacle become an issue in your housing decisions. Remember, without a visa and your *permesso di soggiorno* nothing else matters anyway.

Now, there are some options of finding rentals whereby you never actually live in the space, but you still pay rent to a person for the use of their address. Usually, this will be someone who owns a second home or has an extra room with permission to rent it out and doesn't mind offering you their address. I cannot speak on the moral/ethical side of this, but it is an option.

No matter how you do it, whether finding somewhere to rent either temporarily or to eventually buy, it can be done fairly simply. Just be sure to check everything is acceptable for your visa/*permesso* applications with the powers that be to ensure that there aren't any hiccups along the way.

DAILY LIVING

So, phew, you've made it through the red tape and feel like now you can start to settle into a way of life in Umbria. Obviously, we cannot provide an exact estimate of how much it will cost one to live as it greatly depends on your individual needs. However, this section is just to give you an idea of places to go for your daily needs and how to appreciate what is available as it will undoubtedly differ from home.

Groceries

Grand supermarkets as known in the US or wholesale outlets like Costco are nearly non-existent in Italy, especially in the smaller towns of Umbria. While some larger cities might have a shopping center that houses a larger grocery story like Conad or Coop, it will be hard to find even a large Carrefour around, which are rather common in France. Therefore, you may have to stop at various grocery locations to get items that you are more familiar with at home. This does not always mean that something "cannot be found", but rather it might mean that something "is not so easily accessible".

A common conversation we hear is about the challenge in finding particular spices in the grocery stores. Rest assured that you can find nearly every spice you have ever heard of or used in your cooking, but you may need to buy it online, travel for it, or wait until it comes into stock as not everything is on the shelves all year round. One of the differences that we find lovely about Italian, and most European, grocery stores is that the products - especially produce - are available by seasons.

So far, we have found the following grocery stores:

- **Conad** - There are large stand-alone shops or smaller "express" stores usually in smaller villages.
- **COOP** - Often located with a shopping center or as larger stand-alone shops that are sometimes called "in-Coop".
- **Carrefour Market Express** - like a Conad Express are often smaller 'markets' rather than for a large shop.
- **Pam Local** - These are often located in touristy towns and do not offer a wide variation of daily shopping goods. Locals will likely not shop here, and most residents will only pop in for a quick item or two but use some of the other locales for daily shopping.
- **EuroSpin** - Probably more frequented by expats, these stores are generally located outside of a city center but offer a decent variety of items. You may find more imported products at these shops.
- **Lidl** - Every British expat loves a Lidl. Despite their chaotic organizational characteristic, many may feel a bit of nostalgia and find a variation of items available with their themed sales weeks - like English food, Mexican fiestas, etc.

Of course, there may be other off brand-named grocery marts in the town that you choose to settle in, so don't be afraid to pop in to see what they have on offer as local prices may be a draw for exploring different spots to get your grocery items.

♦ ♦ ♦

I admit that when I first arrived, I only looked for the things that I was used to from my home country. For example, I could never find the spices I wanted to make my chili or roast chicken. However, after speaking with some local expat residents, I was able to find things in different shops. It sometimes means that we have to drive at least 45-minutes to the larger town, like Viterbo, to get imported products at the Conad there, but it is an opportunity to have a day out as well, so I now look forward to it. Anything else that I might really feel I need, I can order from Amazon or other online sites. Of course, I also stock up whenever I visit home or people come to visit us!

~shared by JD

♦ ♦ ♦

Markets

In the US, we might use 'market' to refer to a grocery store or supermarket. However, in Italy *mercato* generally refers to the outdoor markets that are held in a town square somewhere on a weekly, biweekly or monthly basis. While we have yet to find an exhaustive list of all the different town market days/times, just ask your local commune or cafe owner about the times for your commune. It's always fun to see what the locals are buying. Plus, it looks good when expats support their local economy/businesses.

In larger towns, there may be daily *mercatos* that are held in covered areas, so go exploring and find where they are as getting fresh produce or food items is part of the European market and gastronomic adventure.

Online Shops

If you find that you really just cannot live without a particular ingredient or want a little taste of home, then there are some online shops that will satisfy a 'care package' inclination for a price, if you cannot find them on Amazon.it.

- All Ireland Foods
  https://allirelandfoods.ie/
- British Corner Shop
  https://www.britishcornershop.co.uk
- My American Market
  https://www.myamericanmarket.com/us/

Eating out

Unlike many other Western European countries, Italians eat Italian food when they eat out. Therefore, most restaurants are reasonably-priced and serve family-style dishes. After a while, you might find it tiresome to eat Italian food all the time and seek out different cuisine, which is limited, but not impossible to find.

Be prepared to pay more, though. A meal out at an Asian restaurant will cost you close to 40 euros, at least, for two - not including alcohol. Compare that to eating out at an Italian restaurant that will cost you about 20-30 euros for two without alcohol and likely no more than 50 with. Even going out in groups at an Italian eatery will likely be capped at 50 euros per person that includes your drinks and three courses.

Still, as someone once said, "Italian food is great 300 days of the year, but every now and then you want something different."

In that case, there are a fair amount of Asian-fusion (Japanese and Chinese) restaurants around most bigger towns/cities. Some of the more touristy places might have a kebab/hamburger eatery that will cost about 5-10 euros a dish.

So, eating out - especially in local restaurants - will definitely not cost you an arm and leg if you aren't so keen on cooking every day.

For those who do like a bit of a wine-and-dine experience, there are plenty of options available even within the Italian cuisine, but you actually have to seek out those places rather than the other way around.

Shopping

There are outlet malls and shopping centers available for your clothing and retail therapy needs. However, the American-style shopping mall is harder to find outside of Rome or Florence. Within Umbria, your best bet might be in Perugia or a visit to an outlet mall. Familiar store brands like American Eagle, Gap, H&M, Zara, etc. will require a visit to a larger town, or online.

The biggest obstacle, for most, will be finding the right sizes. It would be wise to check the size conversion charts online to ensure that you know your size when you pop into a shop. For ladies, especially, keep in mind that bra sizes are measured completely differently. Stores that are familiar with expat shoppers may be able to help with size conversions, but to save the headache, fear, frustration or any other obstacle that may prevent you from stepping inside a store and having a new experience, just make a note and keep it with you when you decide you want to venture into the Italian fashion scene.

Prices will probably be higher than you might be used to if you usually shop for the more familiar brands. However, the "throwaway" culture is less prevalent in Europe and Italy. Therefore, you'll generally find higher quality pieces that are intended to endure a few seasons of fashion.

Most importantly, have an open mind. Boutique shops are fun, and you never know what gem you might find!

SEEING UMBRIA: TRANSPORTATION

By Air

The only airport in Umbria is in Perugia (PEG). The San Francesco d'Assisi airport https://airport.umbria.it/ita/ connects travelers to about a dozen domestic and international destinations. For visitors from the UK, London Stansted and limited Heathrow flights will go direct into Perugia. RyanAir is the main airline through this airport.

A major advantage of the San Francesco d'Assisi airport is the cheaper overnight parking of about 11 euros per day for the first two days and then decreased amounts every two days thereafter. If you are a regular traveler with overnight or short trips back and forth, then you can get an annual or six-month pass for 600 or 300 euros, respectively. Another plus for this airport is the quick in and out for checking in and immigration processes. While the drive there is not as straight of a shot as the Rome airports, it could be worth your while to give the San Francesco d'Assisi airport a try.

By Train

Most of the larger towns in Umbria have train stations. The big towns will likely have "fast" trains connecting them to Rome or Florence via the main trainline, TrenItalia.

http://bit.ly/3lIPC3j Your best bet for checking on the convenience and feasibility of traveling by train is using an app like Trainline, https://www.thetrainline.com/ which can be used for traveling throughout Europe. Or, more locally, the Moovit app/site https://bit.ly/3XDXQHd will show you the national lines for Perugia and Umbria.

While trains can be convenient, keep in mind that many of the hilltop towns of Umbria will not necessarily have train stations. Furthermore, if they do happen to have one, it may or may not be near the town center at all, so be sure to check your maps to locate where the stations are and determine if it is truly the most accessible for your destination of choice.

By Bus

If trains won't get you to where you want to go, then you can also explore the option of taking the bus to various destinations. *BusItalia* is the main company that will take you to and fro many of the main Umbrian towns. This page http://bit.ly/3YGiCap will provide you with the latest time schedule and stops in the towns you may want to visit – it is in Italian only.

♦ ♦ ♦

With the rise in fuel prices and the state of some of the roads, we actually prefer to take the trains these days. Getting to and from Rome or Florence, or even Venice is super easy on the train. Plus, we like that we can kick back and relax as the beautiful scenery rolls by rather than worrying about the crazy Italian drivers or roadworks on the highways. The only challenge is going across borders as those trains are not always as convenient and some east-west routes are not the easiest. Still, we love the trains!

~shared by TF

♦ ♦ ♦

By Car

Undoubtedly, the most convenient way to travel around and see the beautiful towns of Umbria is by car. It goes without saying, but I'm saying it anyway, you'll have more freedom with your time and ability to see some of the sites off the beaten track.

Of course, there are some potential obstacles to overcome with traveling by car. The most obvious being dependent on your visa type and whether or not you need a local license and/or insurance. Revisit the section about *Driving In Italy*, if you aren't sure about this step.

Assuming all is well and sorted with licensing and insurance matters, then you have a few options when it comes to getting around by car. One, you can rent a car. Two, you can buy a car with some caveats, paperwork and bureaucracy involved. Three, you could try to find a long-term resident/friend who has an extra car you can borrow from time to time.

For short-term residents and even longer-term ones who might not want to wade through the bureaucratic paperwork, renting a car might be the simplest option. It can also be a temporary one until you feel more grounded and settled in getting everything else situated with your new Italian life. I don't have any insights on this other than if you can find a local rental agency, you will likely save more than if you go through the more familiar Western companies. Many of the local agencies will have at least one person on staff willing to plod through in English with you if your Italian is not yet up to snuff. So, don't let the language barrier deter you from the chance to save a few more euros a month and have a more local experience.

While more details on purchasing a car will come in a later volume of this series, just note that it is possible for those on one of the long-term visas with established residency, finances, and health insurance. Just remember that it is another form of bureaucracy and will require you to tap into your well-developed zen mastery.

Finally, there are car-sharing services like BlaBlaCar, https://www.blablacar.it/ or car services for airport shuttles and private events. A list of a few Umbrian ones is provided in the Resources section.

By Bicycle/Motorcycle/Moped

For the two-wheel enthusiasts, who feel the desire to conquer the Umbrian hills, you can obviously get around on one of the two-wheel forms of transportation. There are places to rent bicycles along *Lago di Bolsena* (Lake Bolsena). Also, going into the off-season, you can purchase the likes of an e-bicycle for cheaper than new as the renting companies update their own stock.

As for the other modes of two-wheel transportation, I must admit that I have little to no knowledge about them since this is yet another area of imbalance for me to add to my growing list of "avoid at all costs or injury will be guaranteed!" **Therefore, if one of my fortunate readers has information to add for this section, by all means, please get in touch!**

Must-see Umbrian day trips
- Assisi
- Orvieto
- Perugia
- Spoleto
- Terni
- Todi

Must-do activities
- Lake Bolsena
- Farm to Table dining experience

Seasonal Events
- Umbria Jazz
- Opera
- Orvieto Sound (music)

CONCLUSION

This *Umbria on a Whim Volume 1: The Basics* has hopefully been helpful in getting you started on the process of making your move. Although it may seem daunting, it is well worth it once all of the red tape has been gotten through. My apologies if the tone of this volume is a tad heavy, but I wanted to be sure to not sugar-coat the reality of the bureaucracy and formalities required to settle in. Once everything is done, then *la vita dolce* is truly about sitting back, soaking up the warm sun rays with a glass or bottle of vino in your hand.

As stated in the introduction, there is no doubt that some aspects have been missed. I welcome feedback and conversation for future editions/updates as this is only the beginning of the series. It would be great to hear more stories from those who have already made the move successfully to include as well, so feel free to get in touch at theoshwriter@gmail.com.

Thanks for reading and remember that following your whims can lead you to making your dreams a reality!

Let me leave you with this final anecdote from one of our dear friends.

◆ ◆ ◆

An old Asian proverb says, "Better to see something once than to hear about it a thousand times" and there is so much to see in our adopted country if we lived to be 100, we'd still be discovering the wonderful!

One of the reasons we chose Umbria, and in particular the Orvieto area, is that the location is perfect. It's so easy to reach many other fascinating places by train or car. The most economical way to get about is to take the train when visiting the major cities, but to visit the smaller hilltop towns and lakes, often off the beaten path places, you definitely need a car!

When we moved to Italy full time, we imported our car from the UK, so we now have an Italian registration plate, but a car with the steering wheel on the right which has occasionally been known to confuse the carabinieri (state police) when we are pulled over for routine checks, something which is common here in Italy.

Prior to that, we would travel and day trip in a rental car. Our idea of heaven is to simply potter around a hilltop town and eat great Italian food and wine in a local trattoria. So, one beautiful autumn weekend our "gastronomic getaway" took us to the perfectly preserved Renaissance town of Lucca in northern Tuscany.

Two things which you quickly learn when living in Italy is to expect the unexpected and that signage of any type is kind of limited!

Arriving early, we parked on a wide leafy, tree-lined boulevard just outside the huge walls which surround the historic centre and strolled into the centre of town. After exploring for the morning, we sat at a pavement café and partook of the age-old pastime of people watching, while trying to decide where to eat lunch. The sun was shining, church bells rang out and all seemed well with the world.

Several hours later and with that warm fuzzy feeling that follows a delicious Italian lunch, we set off to walk back to our car. As we left the city walls and onto the boulevard, probably a 15-minute walk, we seemed to be walking much further than when we had arrived that morning. In one horrible moment of realisation, we realised that our rental car was no longer parked where we had left it. And worse than that, when we stepped from the pavement into the road, we could see that there were no cars at all where previously it had been car lined.

Our first thought was of course that it had been stolen, but we quickly realised that actually it had been towed away ... A small warning triangle sat perched on the grassy kerb with a symbol of a tow truck and nothing more, no telephone number, no company name, no clue!

Not to worry I said confidently, we'll ask a passerby! The kindness of strangers in Italy never ceases to surprise me and the Signor we asked for assistance was no exception! His suggestion was the tourist information office in the Centro, but first he declared "We must take a coffee!"

Fortified with caffeine, he accompanied us to the Tourist Information office, which you guessed it, was shut on Sunday afternoon.

It started to drizzle with rain. Our good Samaritan had to carry on his way, and we stood in the huge Piazza wondering what we should do now. Two things then occurred simultaneously, a horse and carriage decked out for a wedding swung into the Piazza and came to a stop near to us and a tour guide arrived with a group of Americans, so we asked her to help. Whilst sympathetic to our situation, she was not from Lucca herself, so she couldn't help, but our conversation was overheard by the gentleman on the horse drawn carriage and he dismounted like one of the three Musketeers and immediately took charge of the situation in his perfect English.

Apparently, there was a football match being played that afternoon and so all of the cars on the avenue had to be gone by 15.00, which locals knew, but all the rental cars of unsuspecting tourists had been towed away.

And boy was he mad about visitors to his City being shown la brutta figura in this way! He whipped two mobile phones from his waistcoat and simultaneously began ringing the local police and car pounds to locate our car, which he did in under 5 minutes flat, all the while the super shiny black horse, dressed in white ribbons stood patiently by.

"I've found your car! But it is not here in the Old City, but I can give you the address," Tomasso declared.

My heart sank, "How will we get there?" I asked.

"I will take you, of course!" said Tomasso, "in my carriage!"

I looked at my husband and he looked back at me ... I was thinking we may have to sell a kidney to pay for this ride. "That's very kind, how much will it be?" I asked.

"€15,00 is fine," said Tomasso.

"Get in!" I gleefully mouthed to B.

It stopped raining and the sun came out, a click of his voice, and we set off at a trot across the cobblestones, the perfect white plume bouncing atop the horse's head. We headed left and right down narrow medieval streets where elderly Italians were sat outside their homes passing the time. I should add that we were dressed extremely casually, like tourists out for the day, with our

wet hair plastered to our heads from the rain shower. Neverthe-
less, given the beautiful horse and carriage adorned with the
wedding decorations, many locals assumed we were just mar-
ried and shouted "Complimenti e auguri" in congratulations as
we passed by. We smiled at each other, and Tomasso laughed
and laughed!

We passed under an old archway and out of the Old City
into three lanes of modern traffic, passed through traffic lights
and around islands at a brisk trot, cars to the left and right of us
... I count this as one of my most surreal and precious memories
of our life in Italy.

Finally, we pulled up at the car pound on a side street. A
guy dressed in a fluorescent yellow jacket was just locking up,
but Tomasso quickly put him in the picture, and we were let in-
side after waving Tomasso off. Our rental car was driven out of
the pound, and we returned to the office to pay the fine which
was €60,00! In my best Italian of that time, I explained how
cross we were to have our car towed away and to pay a fine for
no fault on our part. The Signor listened patiently until I ran out
of Italian, then he winked at me and said, "But Signora, I only
drive the truck!"

~shared by MB

♦ ♦ ♦

REFERENCES

Facebook Groups
- Expats in Italy
  https://www.facebook.com/groups/AnyexpatITALY/
- All About Italy
  https://www.facebook.com/groups/373146790597471
- Expats in Umbria
  https://www.facebook.com/groups/470495779655816
- Expats in Umbria and Lazio
  https://www.facebook.com/groups/expatsUmbriaLazio
- Overseas Property in Italy
  https://www.facebook.com/groups/1806354553019397/

Thank you to these sites (in no particular order) for their information that helped me put this handbook together:
- https://www.livinginumbria.com/why/
- https://www.true-umbria.com/moving-to-umbria-italy/
- https://www.expat.com/forum/viewforum.php?id=334
- https://www.expat.com/forum/334-17-removal-umbria.html
- https://www.gate-away.com/blog/buying-home-in-umbria-take-the-plunge-you-wont-regret-it/
- https://issimoissimo.com/italianissimo/umbria/bellini-travels-guide-to-umbria/
- https://www.walksofitaly.com/blog/travel-tips/how-to-get-around-umbria-italywith-public-transport

- http://www.umbriantravel.com/
- https://www.italiarail.com/umbria
- https://www.regione.umbria.it/salute/aziende-sanitarie-regionali

RESOURCES

Legal Services

- Avvocato Anna Marcella Giardini (office in Fabro)
  Marcella Giardini
  Tel. 0763/832453 | Fax 0763.305313 |
  mobile 3498706574
  giardini@studiogiardini.eu

- *Barbara De Benedittis Relocation and Legal in Italy*
  (Office in Rome, but help for all of Italy)
  Barbara De Benedittis
  badebenedittis@gmail.com

Explore Umbria

- Unspoilt Umbria
  https://www.thebluewalk.com/walking-vacation-in-umbria/
  Mandy Bell (@unspoiltumbria)
  mandy.orvieto@gmail.com

Car Services

- Umbria Chauffeur
  https://www.umbriachauffeur.com/en/
- Umbria Transfer
  https://www.umbriatransfer.com/

AUTHOR BIO

Tara OSH lives with her husband, two Beagles, and two cats in their dream home that was found and purchased on a whim during a visit to Umbria, Italy. Born in South Korea, adopted and raised in Oregon, USA, Tara OSH merges her international persona not only in name, but also as a global citizen. Formerly a professional English language educator, which provided the freedom to travel the world, she now writes to share her experiences in hopes of helping others. She is also proof that even the greatest planners among us can spontaneously make our dreams a reality.